MIDLANDS

The *Midlands Digest* is a series of companions to *A Shropshire Gazetteer* and *Staffordshire and the Black Country*. They contain articles on people and places of interest in an area extended to include the *Potteries and the Peak,* the *Welsh Borders* and the *South Cheshire Plain.* But here the usual sweet mix of beauties and curiosities is leavened with a measure of life today: stories of cruelty and kindness, scandals and skulduggery, laced with a dash of humour

Michael Raven

ISBN 0 906114 18 7

*Front cover:
shire horses on Whixall Moss
photograph M.Raven
5.2.90*

Published by:	Michael Raven 26 Church Lane Derrington Stafford ST18 9LY Tel: 0785 55555
First Edition:	Autumn 1992
ISBN:	0 906114 18 7
Copyright:	Text and photographs Michael Raven 1992 © All rights reserved
Printed by:	Halstan & Co.Ltd. Amersham, Bucks.

FOREWORD

This is the third book in this series. All that was said in the forewords to the previous volumes still stands except in one small regard, that is, that I now frequently use Ilford XP2 film for the photographs. This produces a black and white negative that can be processed and printed by mass production colour machines.

I cannot pretend to get other than the greatest of enjoyment in researching these little books. Each trip is an adventure. Even the actual writing is less of a chore than it was when compiling the big gazetteers.

I am still accompanied almost everywhere by my dogs and make no apology for their appearance in many of the photographs. Indeed, their inclusion can be justified on the technical grounds that they help the reader to judge scale, and that they often fill a hole in the foreground of the pictures, especially when a wide angle lens has been used.

Finally, I am aware that in this series of books I have granted myself a privilege enjoyed by few people, namely, a public platform from which to express private opinions. Those with privileges have a duty to exercise them responsibly and I do my best to be fair to those whom I criticize. As to my facts, I never write anything that I cannot substantiate with either documents or tape recordings.

TIME TO TAKE A BOW

Black Country Towns and Villages
What makes this book really special is the quality of the photographs. They are truly splendid. Michael Raven has the eye which can see beauty in the commonplace, the dismal and the devastated and the skill to communicate it to the rest of us.
John Ogden, Express and Star, 21.4.92

A Shropshire Gazetteer
It must be the definitive book on Shropshire.
The Shropshire Alternative

Dedicated to:
my very good friends
Pirate and Bruno

CONTENTS

S.A.D.P.A.L.S 6
Pirate 9
Boseley Cloud 10
Trescott Cottage 12
Swan Lane Gasometers 13
Hug Bridge 14
Stourton Castle 16
Endon Well Dressing 18
Whitmore Shooting Party 20
Flash Locks on the River Severn 22
Stoke Sewers 24
Culling Foxhounds 26
Tong Swans 27
Continental Raiders 28
Earl Harroby's Private Station 30
Derrington Winter Scene 31
Bike Gang Gun Feud Violence 32
End Hell of Bikers 33
Kibblestone Camp 34
Pirate and Tess 36
Seisdon 38
Exhibit from Outer Space 40
Shropshire County Ranger 42
Alfred Ward of Whixall 43
Bovine Walking Frame 44
A Threat to Kill 45
Astley's Ride 48
Dog and Lampost pub sign 51
Barthomley 52
Kevin Barry O'Donnell 58
Wilbroughton Hall 60
Index 62

S.A.D.P.A.L.S
Stafford and District People's Animal Lifeline Society

Cindy one of the six strays adopted by Mrs Hodson herself

"Once you start you can't stop"; not if you have the heart of gold that belongs to Mrs Hilda Hodson, of Derrington near Stafford. In 1977 she started rescuing and re-homing abandoned and unwanted cats and dogs. She continues this good work, though now well into her retirement years.

To assist her Mrs Hodson has gathered together a small band of dedicated helpers. Two of these work virtually full time: Audrey Cope, director of fund raising; and Leslie Cope, who is responsible for rescueing dogs and puppies. Mrs Hodson looks after the cats and kittens. Between them they save some 250 animals each year.

These three ladies are supported by a number of sympathizers who help with fund raising and fostering animals until they have been found new homes. However, commercial kennels still have to be used, and, even though the owners offer reduced rates,

Mrs Hodson and Penny (above) and Muffin, a 26 year old Burman

kennel fees are a major drain on resources. Unlike most animal care organizations SADPALS never put an animal down. Once a cat or dog is in their hands it stays alive. Some large or old dogs can be difficult to re-house and are costly to keep. So be it. They do not put animals down. In a world full of pheasant shooters, fox hunters and badger baiters these ladies shine like stars in the night.

What is more, even when an animal has been re-housed their interest does not end there. If it is a bitch they will contribute financially to have it neutered; and all new owners are contracted to return the cat or dog to SADPALS if, for any reason, they are unable to continue to keep it.

What with vets' bills, food, transport, advertising and telephone charges, not to mention the hundreds of hours spent locating suitable new owners, it is a miracle that these ladies manage to keep up their good work. Any reader who wishes to help them with time, money, pet food or transport, or who can donate items which can be sold to raise funds, such as homegrown produce, unwanted presents, handicrafts, house plants etc., should contact: Hilda Hodson on Stafford (0785) 42770 or Audrey and Lesley Cope on Stafford 54115.

Two more of Mrs Hodson's strays. Below is Gizmo

Twiggy, a rare Affenpinscher

My dog Pirate, son of Lady, a Border Collie cross, and Ben, a pedigree Rottweiller (1.11.89)

In Memorium

*Stranger you're wrong,
She cannot be dead.
She lies but asleep,
In the sons that she bred.*

Michael Raven 6.1.1990

BOSELEY CLOUD

BOSELEY CLOUD rears up dramatically to a rocky summit and overlooks the Cheshire Plain. Travellers on the many main roads that meet at Congleton will know it well.

The name Cloud is from the Anglo-Saxon *clud,* meaning 'rocky hill'. This rocky hill is now in the care of the National Trust and can be climbed with ease from a small carpark on Cloudside at SJ.707.637, but beware of the precipitous northern faces. The Ordnance Survey trigonometrical point at the summit is 343 metres above sea level; the plain below is at 100 metres.

There are long views in all directions, but especially to the north-west over the Cheshire Plain to Merseyside and Wales. The tall tower on Croker Hill to the north-east is a British Telecom relay station. The village in line with this and the Cloud is Boseley, and the lake beyond the village is Boseley Reservoir.

The Cloud consists of hard, coarse sandstones called 'mill-stone grits' that range in colour from pale grey to red. From time to time these have been quarried for stone to build houses and walls and especially for local works of engineering such as the Macclesfield Canal and the imposing viaduct that carries the railway over the River Dane. There used to be four unusual points called Sugar Rock, Raven Rock, Mareback and Bully Thrumble. The latter was a 65 foot corkscrew pillar.

The Cloud seems such an obvious place for prehistoric man to have built a fort-settlement that it comes as a surprise to learn that there is little hard evidence for one. Two sections of a curved ditch cut out of the rock - one 790 feet long, the other 180 feet - were described in 1878, but hill forts on land that has been quarried are often destroyed. The shallow, square entrenchment at SJ.900.634, in the conifer trees on the west of the hill, is of debatable origin. Some authorities think that it might be an Iron Age fort, but others believe it to be of comparitively late origin, a forestry plantation enclosure perhaps.

The long southern slopes, called Black Heath, are heather moor with a little pasture. They run down to Dial Lane, part of the Earlsway, the route taken by the medieaval earls of Chester when they visited their estates in Leek and beyond.

Adjacent to Dial Lane are the Bridestones, a much reduced but still impressive Neolithic (about 2,500 BC) burial chamber at SJ.906.622. For more on the Bridestones see *Staffordshire and the Black Country* by M Raven, p34, and *Walks in Mysterious Cheshire* by Tony Bowerman, pp137-8.

Boseley Cloud from the south-east. Stone from quarries on the hill was used by Thomas Telford in the construction of the Macclesfield Canal, opened in 1831. The 12 locks that straddle the A54 are well known to boatsmen. Boseley Reservoir was opened in 1832 as a feeder for the canal (12.2.92)

TRESCOTT
This rare little timber-framed and thatched cottage stands beside the Wolverhampton to Bridgnorth road. The name Trescott means 'the cottage by the Tressel', the old name of the Smestow Brook (4.2.92)

Swan Lane gasholders, West Bromwich (17.2.88)

HUG BRIDGE

HUG BRIDGE carries the Macclesfield to Leek road over the River Dane at SJ.981.636. It has always been an important crossing, especially as the Dane marks the boundary between Cheshire and Staffordshire. (Dane is from *Dana*, the wife of the Celtic sky god *Lud.*) The original timber bridge of 'tottering poles' collapsed in 1620 and soon after was rebuilt in stone. The present red sandstone bridge is also in the process of slowly collapsing and the retaining walls are heavily buttressed on the downstream side.

The name Hug is thought to be a survival of the original pronunciation of Hugh, from Hugh Despencer. He was a Norman knight who came over with William the Conqueror and whose family held sway in these parts for much of the Middle Ages.

During the last five years North West Water have been busy on both sides of the bridge. First they drilled two boreholes but these have had to be abandoned because the subterranean waters contained unacceptably high levels of metallic salts; then they built a weir (a low dam) to draw water from the Dane itself and an extensive pumping plant. The construction costs exceeded six million pounds and on an average day they abstract one million gallons of water from the Dane.

A mile to the south, at Rushton Spencer (from the Despencers), there are two more boreholes which together provide another two million gallons a day.

Continue south, down the A523, and you will be treated to some of the finest inland water views in England. Lake Rudyard was constructed in 1831 as a feeder reservoir for the Cauldon Canal. That sounds mundane, but this is a beautiful place, whatever the season, whatever the time of day.

For more on Rushton Spencer and Lake Rudyard see *Staffordshire and the Black Country*, by M Raven.

Above: Dave Shaw, resident waterman at Hug Bridge

Top right: looking downstream over the weir to the bridge

Bottom right: The weir and the water extraction point to its right and a small part of the waterworks behind (24.2.92)

STOURTON CASTLE

STOURTON CASTLE (SO.859.849) stands embowered in trees on a bluff above the River Stour, the banks of which are bedecked with fishermen all year round.

There was a fortified Hunting Lodge at Stourton from at least 1184 and King John is known to have hunted in the surrounding Forest of Kinver in 1207 and 1215.

The castellated square stone tower, now smothered in cement render, probably dates from about 1400 and was once protected by a curtain wall with circular towers. Most of the brick ranges are late 16th Century with 17th Century gables. The mock Jacobean west wings date from the 1830's when Sir Robert Smirke altered and restored the building.

Stourton Castle passed through the hands of several medieaval noble families until the construction of a forge on the river in about 1650. Soon after this gentry ceased to live here and the castle became first a farmhouse and then the home of industrialists. Today, the noisy mill is long gone and Stourton is the home of Mr Fred Phillips, the noted breeder and authority on Staffordshire Bull-terriers.

For further information on Stourton Castle see the Victoria County History of Staffordshire, volume 1 p369, and volume 20 pp130-2.

Stourton Castle viewed from the south-east (16.2.92)

MENAGE A TROIS at Whiston Cross, Albrighton, near Wolverhampton. The dog on the right is a working foxhound *(3.1.91)*

Endon Well Dressing

Since 1845 the custom of dressing the village water wells with flower pictures on Spring Bank Holiday Monday has been practiced at the attractive, stone-built settlement of Endon. Endon is just north of the Potteries, on the road to Leek.

The pictures are made by pressing flower petals, seeds and mosses on to the surface of a tray of clay.

The event is well(!) attended and there are a variety of entertainments: sporting competitions, a fun fair, Morris dancing, side stalls and a gipsy fortune teller. The high point is the crowning of the May Queen. In fact she is crowned four times, which is, we think, three times too often.

The 1989 Well Dressing display at Endon

The 1989 May Queen photographed as she crosses the footbridge over the stream near the centre of Endon during the Well Dressing celebrations

WHITMORE SHOOTING PARTY

We were driving home on a grey winter's afternoon. There were roadworks at Whitmore and the traffic came to a standstill. On the hill to our left there was a line of men with shotguns spread some 35 yards apart. In the woods on the horizon came the distant clatter of men shouting, dogs barking and sticks being thwacked against trees. A few terrified birds flew out of the wintry woods.

We left the car and entered the field. Gunmen fired erratically at the high-flying pheasant and partridge. Most of the birds escaped, but nearby a luckless creature plummeted from the sky and crashed on to the frosty ground. It was retrieved by a spaniel. But only the dog was excited. The men looked bored.

A whistle blew, guns were put in bags and the unusually large party of shooters and beaters plodded desultorily to their battered Toyotas. The young squire, a grandson of the aged incumbent of Whitmore Hall, nervously questioned our presence and eyed our cameras with suspicion. It was the end-of-season shoot and on this day the beaters were shooters and the shooters were beaters – the officers serving the men. They were a humourless lot and when they spoke they avoided looking you in the eye.

Master Mainwearing (right), grandson of the the present squire, and two gunmen at Whitmore (1.2.92)

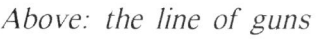

Above: the line of guns

Right: cold blooded, a gunman poses at Whitmore

Below: the spaniels handle the fallen birds with gentleness
(1.2.92)

FLASH LOCKS on the River Severn

In his book, *The Worst Journey in the Midlands*, Sam Llewellyn humorously describes his journey from the source of the Severn to London by river and canal using first a canoe and then the row-boat *Magdalen*.

In the extract printed opposite he describes how the old time bow hauliers traversed un-navigable stretches of the Severn, a notoriously treacherous river that was prone to lose water overnight and leave large cargo ships stranded on shallow reaches.

Pubished in 1983
by William Heineman Ltd
SBN 434 42745 4

*There's Peter O'Malley
and Jessie and Jem;
None finer you'll find
As bow haulier men.*

Sam Llewellyn was born in the Isles of Scilly in 1948. Educated at Eton and Oxford, he has spent time as a publisher in London, a wilderness hand in Canada, and a novelist in Ireland. He now lives in Shropshire with his wife, two children, banjoes, and boats.

The navigation of the upper Severn is a tribute to human muscle power. Nowadays the limit of navigation is at Bewdley, some miles downstream from the gorge. Once, the barges went all the way up to Pool Quay and beyond. Pool Quay is nearly at Welshpool, miles of rapids and shallows from the sea.

Rivers are kept up with weirs, which dam up the water to make it deep enough for boats to float. Weirs are usually found in association with locks – all pound locks nowadays, with a gate at either end and sluices you crank up and down to fill or empty them. These are a fairly recent invention; they are also astonishingly expensive to build. A cheaper, more primitive and generally coarser solution is the flash lock.

To build an impromptu flash lock you need about eighty men and a river. A boat is optional, serving the purpose of providing a reason for building the lock in the first place. The boat, if used, is towed as far up the river as current and depth allow. When it grinds to a halt, the men collect rocks and trees and, in the case of the rougher crews, cottages and farm carts, and bung them into the river to form a dam. It is a very rapid river that falls a foot in a mile; so if you can raise the water level two feet, you gain plenty of ground. Travelling upstream, you have to wait for the river to back up. Travelling downstream, you cruise up to your dam and break it down. The resulting lump of water is known as the 'flash', and the idea is to stay aboard it until the diverging banks have lowered it to the point where you are bumping the bottom again.

On most of the waterways of England, horses were the motive power. On the Severn, however, human beings were used, because they did not need a towpath and also because it was found that horses made lousy flash weirs, at least when alive. This caused terrible suffering to people of conscience, and many efforts were made to relieve the poor man-haulers. These were eventually successful, at which the first towpath between Gloucester and Shrewsbury was built. The man-haulers rioted with horrible violence. Nobody had consulted them, and it transpired that they looked on the whole thing as an excuse to be paid for getting some fresh air, not to mention money, rum, pheasants, wenches and anything else not nailed down by the riverside. But as usual, nobody paid any attention to them. So one meets few, if any, on the Severn now.

STOKE SEWERS

It hardly bears thinking about and politicians do their best to forget, but Britain's sewers are badly in need of replacement. The task is immense, vastly expensive and fraught with problems. The people of Boothen, Stoke on Trent, have some idea of the horrors in store for the rest of us.

Severn Trent Water started to replace their sewers in early summer, 1991. In January, 1992, the Evening Sentinel reported:

"Progress has been slow as workmen have hit countless setbacks. Families say they could never have forseen the scale of devastation and disruption caused by the works.

Businesses have lost vital trade caused by traffic diversions and scores of householders have seen cracks develop in their subsidence hit homes.

Lonsdale Street became an 'unforgiveable eyesore' and property owners complained about mud and the stench of sewage.

In the most serious incident a drain collapsed in Boothen Road a week before Christmas. Two homes in Nicholls Street and Windsmoor Street had to be evacuated for safety and are still shored up by scaffolding."

The work continues but in the meantime householders have held a public meeting and Severn Trent have promised to make early compensation payments.

Replacing the sewers at the corner of Boothen Road and Windsmoor Street, Stoke (23.12.91)

CULLING FOXHOUNDS

At about the age of seven years all foxhounds are shot dead. Despite having a genuine affection for their hounds kennelmen regularly decapititate the dead dogs, discard the heads and then butcher the bodies to feed back to the pack. Feeding 80 or more hounds is an expensive business and nothing is wasted. In the photograph a hound's head lies amongst the offal and other inedible parts of fallen livestock used to feed the hounds. It was taken from a video made at a north Midland hunt kennel abattoir.

Furthermore, we have two witnesses with hunt connections who have seen one local kennelman butcher the bodies of unwanted foxhound pups and feed them back to their mothers.

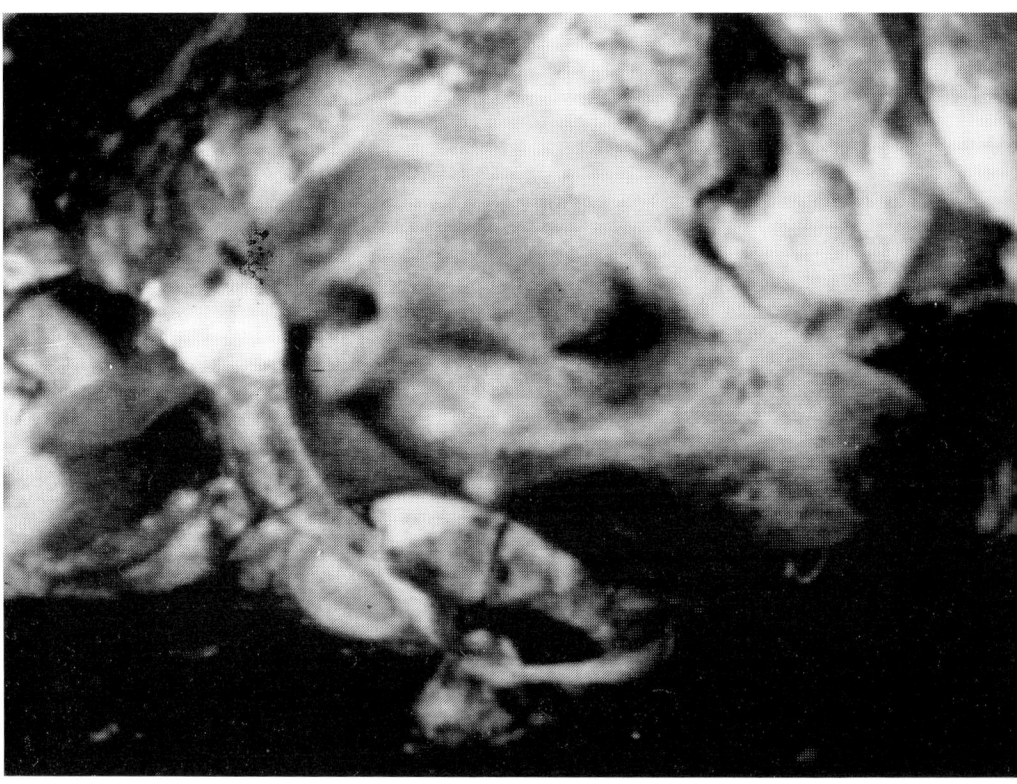

The discarded head of a culled foxhound

Tong, a family of swans on the lake opposite the church
(6.8.87)

28 Continental Raiders

Downton Castle, near Ludlow, now owned by a Greek millionaire.

To foster their pheasants
They killed all the cats
Did that French Madam Prima
And her gun happy keeper

True, it was a local scandal
and the gamekeeper was fired.

Bringewood Forge, near Ludlow, now owned by a French millionairess.

Earl Harroby's Private Station

In 1849 the second Earl of Harroby had this little neo-Jacobean station at Sandon (near Stafford) built for his personal use.

It is constructed of brick with stone dressings and comes complete with tall chimneys and a porte-cochere.

The station was renovated recently but trains no longer stop here. The premises are presently in the care of Bow Bells, architectural carpenters.

Winter scene near Derrington, Stafford. The stream is a tributary of the Doxey Brook (c.1991)

Bike gang feud gun violence

SHOTGUNS were fired outside the headquarters of the Stafford Eagles as a feud with a rival motor cycle gang exploded into violence, a jury heard this week.

Eagles allegedly kidnapped rival

John Snell, prosecuting, claimed a serious disturbance took place outside the gang's clubhouse in Stone Road, because the Eagles had allegedly kidnapped a member of the Cheshire-based Chosen Few.

The jury at Stafford Crown Court were told that members of the Chosen Few and helpers came down to Stafford to free Ray Martin.

One carload chased a van suspected of being involved in the kidnap at high speed along the A34, with shots being fired at it. When the chase led to the Stone Road clubhouse, more shots were fired and vehicles damaged, although no-one was hurt.

One woman neighbour looked out of her window to find a gun being aimed at her, said Mr Snell.

The trouble started when the Eagles took exception to Ray Martin drinking in pubs in Stafford. The bikers were 'very territorial' and after pleas to the president of the Chosen Few were rebuffed, the Stafford Eagles decided to kidnap Mr Martin from his home in Shelton, Stoke-on-Trent to give him a fright.

When the Chosen Few heard about it, two of them got shotguns and went looking for Mr Martin. Meanwhile his father, pub landlord Reg Martin, was also told about the incident and asked three of his customers to help him.

Two cars containing a total of nine men came down to Stafford, although only one was involved in chasing the white van.

The event took place on 4.9.91; the court case Feb. 1992

After the incident the cars headed back towards Stoke-on-Trent. One of the guns was ditched in a layby on the A34. Police, alerted by a phone call, tailed Reg Martin's car back to his pub, where he and four others were arrested.

The others were picked up later, although Johnson only gave himself up a few weeks ago.

Phillip Leeke, 28, of Newcastle Road, Brereton, Rugeley; Reg Gibson, 21, of Keepers Fold, Middlewich, Cheshire and Christopher Johnson, 35, of Nantwich Road, Wimbolsley, Middlewich all admitted violent disorder. Leeke and Johnson also admitted possessing a loaded shotgun in a public place.

Those convicted of violent disorder by the jury were: Reg Martin, 50, formerly of the Mail Coach Public House, Cliffe Vale, Stoke-on-Trent, now of Leach Avenue, Chesterton, and Gordon Upton, 31, of Elizabeth Street, Crewe, the 'chairman' of the Chosen Few.

Jury told of terrifying disturbance outside Eagles' clubhouse

Eagles are 'gentlemen' says landlord
End 'hell' of bikers

Neighbours of the notorious Stafford Eagles clubhouse on the Stone Road are calling for the bikers to be evicted to put an end to 'three years of hell'.

But landlord Michael Raven says he has no intention of asking them to leave and described them as 'gentlemanly'.

The call comes after a rival faction of bikers descended on the clubhouse in the early hours of Wednesday last week, firing gun shots at the fortified building.

But Mr Raven, who lives in the Ashley area, near Market Drayton, said his own experience of the bikers was good.

He claimed that up until this week nobody had ever complained to him about the residents of 263, Stone Road and that he was not aware of any problems.

"They have always been courteous, never used bad language and were always very gentlemanly when I have had dealings with them," he said.

"As far as I am concerned, things can't have been that bad or people would have complained before."

●The Eagles''fortress'

And he added: "It doesn't seem fair to me to ask them to leave when they were the ones who were under attack in the first place."

Stafford Post 12.9.91

Kibblestone Camp

In 1868 Richard Pirie Copeland, of the famous Spode pottery family, came to Kibblestone. He built the Hall, complete with ballroom, around the nucleus of an old farmhouse. Ronald Copeland was born at the mansion in 1884.

He was a friend of Lord Baden Powell and formed one of the first scout groups in the country at the village of Oulton, 1½m NE of Stone. He also leased land on his picturesque estate for a permanent camp site. This continues, and indeed is famous throughout the world. It is situated in a wooded valley with several permanent brick and stone buildings, rocky outcrops, a plunge pool, flowery dells and stands of specimen trees. In 1935 Ronald's mother, Emily, died and the Hall remained empty until it was demolished shortly after the end of the Second World War. However, the family is still resident on the estate; Spencer Copeland lives at Kibblestone Park, close by the site of the old Hall.

Kibblestone Hall, demolished after the war

Totem-pole at Kibblestone Camp (27.2.92)

1 Hullo, what's your name?

2 Oh, my goodness it's a Rottweiler disguised with a tail

3 I'm getting out of here

Pirate and Tess

Pirate is my dog, a Rottweiler-Border Collie cross, but as to little Tess, well, her make and model are anybody's guess. She was saved by SADPALS of Stafford.
(Photographs 25.2.92)

4 Mercy! Mercy!

5 I think you're ever so strong and big and handsome

Seisdon   3/4m NW of Trysull

Tucked up against the Shropshire border Seisdon was something of a forgotten place. However, it is now on the route of the Staffordshire Way long-distance footpath and is therefore becoming better known. The name is from the Old English *Seaxes-dun,* 'the hill of the Saxons', probably the 300 foot hill just to the west of the settlement.

Seisdon was one of the five Anglo-Saxon Hundreds of the County of Staffordshire. The other four were Cuttlesdon and Totmonslow in the north, and Afflow and Pirehill in the south. The Hundred was an administrative unit and amongst the duties of its officers were the collection of taxes and enforcement of the law. Although now defunct, some Hundreds were involved in local government into the early years of the 19th Century.

Today, Seisdon is a substantial, spread-about village in the valley of the Smestow Brook. Most of the houses surround an extremely large village green. Only the noisy lorries from the extensive Tarmac sand and gravel quarries on the hill disturb the quiet of this otherwise thriving but peaceful place.

Above: Seisdon Hall. Opposite: the Old Mill House

By the willow-lined brook is an old brick mill and mill house. They bear a plaque 'RW 1749', but there was doubtless a mill here long before that. There are several substantial red brick farms and three 'big houses': the modest but attractive red brick Old Manor House dated 'HE1684' which has two gables, string courses and ball finials; the substantial Seisdon Hall, small red bricks with stone dressings, shaped gables, tall chimneys and reputed to be Elizabethan with a half-timbered core presently occupied by the Foster family and their pack of varied and vociferous dogs; and Seisdon House, 5 bays, low red brick Georgian with a columned porch.

Between the grander houses are an old sandstone cottage, some black and white buildings, the old white-painted Smithy (dated 1787), some pleasant modern houses, a Post Office/general store and the Seven Stars. The modern pub stands on the sight of an ancient hostelry.

Of ancient monuments the Victoria County History records: "On Seisdon Common, near Abbott's or Apwood Castle (3/4m SW of Seisdon), is a small square intrenchment with a single ditch, situated on a round promontory; near the common (1 1/3m S of Seisdon) is a large triangular stone called War Stone, which Mr. Coote suggests is a 'trifinnial boundary stone'; 1 1/4m W of Seisdon at Moat Rough is a dry rectangular moat 177 feet by 143 feet."

exhibit from outer space

● Michael Pace at Newchapel

EVEN readers with only a slight interest in astronomy will surely be as intrigued as I am to hear that a little piece of the planet Mars is coming to North Staffordshire.

This literally far-flung chip of space debris will be arriving any day now at the Natural Sciences Centre at Newchapel, where it will be placed on permanent exhibition.

Director Michael Pace tells me that the rock was originally thought to be an ordinary meteorite when it landed in Africa 30 years ago. But since then it has been identified as Martian through evidence gained from the Viking landing on Mars in 1976.

The rock is coming to Newchapel from America and has been acquired by Michael's twin brother Tony. Its arrival is nicely timed, in view of the project to fire off another exploratory rocket to Mars later this year.

This latest development adds to the interest of the Newchapel site, which has grown dramatically in the last five years and now attracts several thousand visitors annually.

Among many features are a planetarium, a dinosaur display and windmills which generate electricity. Satellite weather pictures from 23,000 miles up in space are received every four minutes on a colour monitor.

The former pit mound has also been converted into a wildlife and conservation area with clay-lined ponds. A television camera will be used this year to display and magnify water creatures.

Evening Sentinel 5.3.92

NEWCHAPEL OBSERVATORY, the result of 25 years' work by Michael Pace (right), pictured here with his assistant Kevin Boyle. The observatory hides behind a row of terraced houses in this dour, hilltop mining village. (7.1.91)

NEWCHAPEL, 1m E of Kidsgrove, north Staffordshire. The bleak moorland view from Saint James's church. James Brindley, the first great canal engineer, is buried here. (7.1.91)

Shropshire County Council Ranger mending a fence on Lyth hill, south of Shrewsbury (4.9.87)

Alf Ward, smallholder and breeder of shire horses, at Whixall Moss, near Whitchurch (5.2.92)

Bovine Walking Frame

Farmer Barry Roberts of Aston Rogers, South Shropshire, had a cow that was crippled with injuries to its back legs. Normally it would have been put down but instead Mr Roberts had a bovine walking frame constructed at a cost of £600. A canvas sling supports the cow's weight and enables it to trundle around under its own steam during the recovery period. The patient appeared to be quite content and could even suckle her calf.
(19.2.92, from pictures transmitted by Central Television)

Barry Robert, left, and his bovine walking frame, below

A THREAT TO KILL

In 1989 I had a personal disagreement with PC John Leigh. Shortly afterwards my dogs were accidentally let out of my cottage by a builder. John Leigh went looking for them with a gun and they were never seen again.

In 1990 I was charged with threatening to kill John Leigh. I denied the offence. The only evidence against me was the uncorroborated allegation of John Leigh.

He had made three previous allegations, all of which I had proved were totally untrue. He had also told several blatant lies, both to his solicitor and other police officers. These falsities are all documented in letters, statements and tape recordings.

This evidence showed John Leigh to be a man of dubious integrity; it also showed that he had a motive for making a false accusation, i.e., that he felt foolish and frustrated at being thwarted in his previous attempts to discredit me.

But my documentary evidence could only be used in court if the witnesses to whom it related attended the court in person. They were all policemen. I asked these officers if they would attend court as witnesses for the defence. They all refused.

WITNESS SUMMONSES

I then applied to the court for Witness Summonses to be issued to compel them to attend. I was turned down on the ground that their evidence was an attack on the integrity of John Leigh and that was not allowed. The man who advised the magistrates on the law was the Clerk to the Court, a Mr M P Benson.

The next day I went to the library and looked up the law in this matter. Mr Benson was wrong. The law is quite clear: *evidence of motive is overriding reason for the issue of a Witness Summons, even if it incidentally discredits the witness.*

I phoned Mr Benson and told him of his mistake. I asked for another hearing. His reply was that he would not let one magistrate sit in judgement of another. My only recourse was to get a Judicial Review and he did not know how to apply for that. I enquired of two local solicitors. They did not know the procedure either.

THE PRICE OF JUSTICE

Finally, the Lord Chancellor's office obliged and put me in touch with a specialist law firm in London. The cost? £1,500 down as a retainer and undisclosed charges to follow. That was the price of justice. I was right, they said, the court should have issued the summons. However, it was unlikely that I would get my costs returned. Why? Because I had acted for myself. A lawyer would have been able to draw the magistrate's attention to the Clerk's ignorance of the law.

I told all this to Mr Benson. He was complacent and totally unashamed that his error would cost me such a large sum to set right. "But I can't afford it", I said. "Then you'll just have to borrow the money", he replied. With that he put the 'phone down and from then on refused to speak to me again.

As a last resort I wrote to the Chief Constable and asked him to allow his officers to attend the court as witnesses for the defence. He did not reply.

THE TRIAL

On the day of my trial none of my police witnesses turned up. You can imagine my disgust. I was able to hint to the magistrates what had happened, but without any evidence to show that my accuser was anything other than an upstanding and truthful man they found me guilty. However, they showed their sympathy for my predicament by fining me a mere £100.

After the trial I went over the Chief Constable's head and complained to the Crown Prosecution Service in London on another, related matter. I now have the satisfaction of knowing that as I write John Leigh is being investigated by a Chief Superintendant and a Detective Chief Inspector on a charge that he committed perjury during my trial. You can get seven years in prison for perjury. The reader might not think it worthy of me to say this, but I hope John Leigh has many sleepless nights. He inflicted an eternity of them on my dogs.

JUDICIAL GOSSIPERS

Whilst waiting for my case to be called during the preliminary hearings I sat on the public benches in the court and listened to other proceedings. I was uncomfortable at what I saw. What disturbed me was this: whenever the magistrates left the court their Clerk – the man who advises them on the law and the penalties they can inflict – and the Crown Prosecutor invariably had a cosy little téte a téte. They knew each other well, saw each other almost every day, shared boring moments together and passed the time with gossip and in-jokes. Rarely was the defence solicitor there. He changed from case to case.

I saw this happen all morning on each of the days I attended the court. I complained both verbally and in writing that what they were doing was very wrong. Could the Clerk be impartial when the Crown Prosecutor was such a close friend? And if so should he not have the common sense to at least keep a dignified distance from the Prosecutor in public?

Mr Benson, the Clerk who is in charge of all the courts at Newcastle, was visibly angry at my observations. "We can be both friendly on a personal level and impartial during a case," he said. "But," I replied, "Justice should not only be done, it should be seen to be done." "I suppose so," he said.

The courts and their officers demand our respect. They do not have it of right. Respect has to be earned.

ASTLEY'S RIDE

PHILIP ASTLEY was a household name in the second half of the 18th Century. He pioneered the circus as a popular entertainment in England, his personal skill being that of a trick rider.

Astley was born at Porthill, Newcastle-under-Lyme, in 1742 and became an apprentice to his father, a cabinet maker. However, at about the age of 17 he joined the cavalry and quickly gained a reputation as an outstanding horseman.

He left the army and set up as a trainer and trick rider. To add variety to his performances he employed clowns (he called them Merrymen), jugglers, acrobats and other troubadour acts who normally worked on the streets and in fairgrounds. For the first time they performed collectively in specially built circular wooden arenas. The circus was born. It was immensely popular both with the ordinary man and with royalty; George III and Marie Antoinette were amongst Astley's admirers.

The English country dance tune called *Astley's Ride* is 18th Century in style and was almost certainly named after Philip Astley, if not specially composed for his circus musicians.

Philip Astley

Astley's Ride English country dance tune

Drawn by Michael Raven

ASTLEY, PHILIP (1742–1814), equestrian performer and theatrical manager, was born at Newcastle-under-Lyme. Receiving little education, he was brought up to his father's trade of cabinet-making and veneer-cutting. About 1759 he joined General Elliott's regiment of light horse, became rough-rider and breaker-in, and rose to the rank of sergeant-major. Having distinguished himself at the battles of Emsdorff and Friedburg and upon other occasions, he obtained his discharge, and opened an exhibition of horsemanship in an open field in Lambeth, his only horse being his regimental charger, given him by General Elliott. He travelled through the country, performing at fairs and markets, resorting sometimes to his old trade as a cabinet-maker. In 1770 he opened a wooden theatre, with sheltered seats, but with an unroofed circus, in a timber-yard at the foot of Westminster Bridge. In 1775 Mr. and Mrs. Astley appeared on horseback at Drury Lane in the jubilee in honour of Shakespeare. The theatre in Lambeth was gradually enlarged and improved, and called the Amphitheatre Riding House. In 1781 the theatre was opened in the evening, and a candle-light exhibition first attempted, the earlier performances having been presented in the daytime. He had no license from the magistrates, but he pretended that his theatre was under the special protection of a royal patent. In 1783 he was committed to prison for performing illegally, but he was released upon the intervention of Lord Chancellor Thurlow, whose daughters had been taught to ride by Astley. Presently the magistrates granted him a license; he now called his theatre the Royal Grove, having painted the interior to resemble foliage, and added a stage to his circus, to vie with the attractions of a rival establishment of like kind opened on the site of the present Surrey Theatre. He carried his performers to Dublin and Paris, and established equestrian theatres in both those cities. In Paris he instituted the cirque known in later times as Franconi's. He endeavoured to establish floating baths on the Thames off Westminster Bridge. The French Revolution interrupted his performances in Paris, and his amphitheatre was converted into barracks. He re-entered the army, and served with distinction under the Duke of York. In 1794 the Royal Grove Theatre was burnt to the ground. Astley obtained leave of absence from the duke, hurried home to rebuild his theatre, and meanwhile engaged the old Lyceum building in the Strand for equestrian performances. His new theatre was opened in 1794, under the patronage of the Prince of Wales and Duke of York, and in 1798 he was permitted to designate his establishment Astley's Royal Amphitheatre. After the peace of Amiens he returned to Paris, presented his claims before the First Consul, regained possession of his premises, and obtained payment of rent for the whole period of their occupation by the troops of the Revolution. With great difficulty he made his escape from Paris upon the issue of the decree for the detention of all English subjects in France. In 1803 the amphitheatre was again destroyed by fire, Astley's loss being estimated at 25,000*l*. Forthwith he laid the first stone of a new building, which was completed in time to open on Easter Monday, 1804. Astley now retired from active management in favour of his son, receiving, however, one clear half of the annual profits. He next attempted to establish an amphitheatre on the Middlesex side of the Thames, and obtaining a license through the influence of Queen Charlotte for 'music, dancing, burlettas, pantomimes, and equestrian exhibitions,' he opened the Olympic Pavilion on the site of the present Olympic Theatre. By this venture he lost 10,000*l*. In 1812 he sold the Olympic Pavilion to Elliston for 2,800*l*. and a small annuity to be paid during the life of Astley. There was but one payment of the annuity. Astley died in Paris, aged 72, and was buried in the cemetery of Père-la-Chaise. His son, 'Young Astley,' also an admired equestrian performer, to whom he had bequeathed the interest arising from his somewhat encumbered property, survived seven years only. He also died in Paris, and was interred beside his father in Père-la-Chaise. Philip Astley was the best horse-tamer of his time. He usually bought his horses in Smithfield, caring, as he said, 'little for shape, make, or colour: temper was the only consideration.' He rarely gave more than five pounds for a horse. He was a man of violent temper, peremptory of speech and rude of manner, but of great energy and notable integrity; and he was regarded with affection by the members of his company. He constructed in all nineteen amphitheatres for equestrian exhibitions.

[De Castro's Memoirs, 1824; Brayley's Theatres of London, 1833.]   D. C.

This is the pub sign of the Dog and Lamp Post, formerly the New Inns, Dudley Road, Brierley Hill. It was painted by John Edwards and depicts a real incident. The dog's name was Mick the Black Country Gnasher, the policeman was Sergeant Bannock, and the place was Hill Street.

Barthomley
One of Cheshire's hidden treasures

Old Hall Farm, Barthomley (24.3.92)

Barthomley is situated 4m SE of Crewe, and only ½m E of Junction 16 on the M6, where the A500 Potteries link road joins the motorway.The village belies this gloomy description, and is, in truth, quite delightful.

We made our approach from the south-east and were greeted by the handsome Old Hall Farm. It is of red brick with half-timbered fascias on the first floor and cast-iron latticed windows. The core of the house is 17th Century, but it has been very much restored. Adjacent to the Hall is a small triangular green with a bright red telephone kiosk surrounded by a host of daffodils.

Continuing towards the centre of the village one passes a fine and externally unrestored row of three cottages. Fir Tree Cottages are half timbered and thatched and were originally one house. Opposite is a group of cream-painted brick Council houses, though they are not the blot on the landscape you might have imagined.

WOLF AND WHITE LION

A stream runs alongside the lane. It is called Wulvarn and legend has it that it was given this name because the last wolf in England was killed on its banks. On its banks today are two splendid willows. They frame to perfection the picturesque centre of the village. Two buildings dominate the scene: the ancient pub and the even more ancient church.

The White Lion (1614), black and white and thatched, is locally well known. Not only is it exceedingly pretty, it is a real ale pub of sufficient standing to have been given a Pub of the Year Award in 1992 by CAMRA. Of the landlord, batchelor Terry Cartwright, it was said: "He has continued a fine tradition of good beer, cheap bar snacks and friendly service." In fact, the White Lion was a private cottage, home of the schoolmaster and later of the Parish Clerk, until the last years of the 19th Century. The name comes from the lion in the Crewe family's Coat of Arms. The original pub, the Punchbowl (or Steps as the locals called it), was built into the churchyard wall, but was demolished in 1867.

SAINT BERTOLINE

The church stands high on a promontory, lording it above the houses huddled below. It is dedicated to Saint Bertoline (or Bertelin), an obscure 8th Century saint who established his own church at Stafford. He was said to have performed a miracle on the spot where Barthomley church now stands. The Domesday Book name of the settlement was Bertemleu, from *Bertoline's leah*. Of the timber-built Anglo-Saxon chapels nothing remains, and only a little of the Norman stone church that replaced them still exists. Of the sandstone structure we see today: the nave is Perpendicular Gothic of the 15th and 16th Centuries, the tower is 15th Century; the 13th Century chancel was rebuilt in 1852

The White Lion, Barthomley, a renowned Real Ale pub

and much altered in 1924; the Crewe Chapel was built by Sir Ranulph Crewe in the 17th Century; the south aisle has a section of small, irregular stones between the windows, which are probably of the 12th Century church; the north aisle has a 16th Century carved oak screen; and the north wall outside has a repositioned Norman doorway with distinctive zig-zag decoration and the small, incomplete head of a green man with foliage hair. Special mention must be made of the most handsome Elizabethan oak altar table. It has two carved panels: the Nativity and the Flight to Egypt which includes a squirrel eating a nut, the 16th Century county emblem of Cheshire.

LOCAL LANDOWNERS

St. Bertoline's was the centre of a large parish which originally included the villages of Balterley, Crewe, Alsager and Haslington. Soon after the Norman Conquest these estates were held by the Praer family. In 1313 Richard Praer married Joanna, daughter of the heiress of Thomas de Crewe. Their granddaughter married Sir Robert Fulleshurst, who was knighted after fighting at the Battle of Poitiers (1356). He inherited the Crewe and Barthomley estates on the death of his wife. During the reign of Elizabeth I the Fullehursts sold these properties to Sir Christopher Hatton, Lord Chancellor of England, and in 1608 Ranulph Crewe bought them back and returned them to the Crewe name.

Around the church is a cluster of black and white cottages with colourful, well tended gardens. Some are Victorian estate houses but, no matter; they are of interest in their own right. In the countryside around are farms with pretty names: Walnut Tree, Toad Hole, Foxley and Daisy Bank. To the south-east is the

The handsome 11th Century Norman doorway rebuilt in the north wall of the church of Saint Bertoline at Barthomley

sleepy, red brick hamlet of Engelsea-brook. This is famous for its Primitive Methodist Chapel (1828). Hugh Bourne and William Clowes, the founders of the sect, often preached in the village and there is a small museum in the chapel (open 2.00 to 4.30 pm April to September).

CLOGS AND CHOSTS

Recently a new, old trade came to Barthomley when Joe Horrocks set up as a clog-maker in an outbuilding of the White Lion. But the living have competition from the dead at Barthomley. What is now the Rectory was once the Hall, a two-storey Georgian house beside the church. It used to have a third floor, the haunt of the ghost of Randle Crewe.

CIVIL WAR MASSACRE

More dread is the presence of the 12 souls of local people massacred on the floor of the church tower in 1643, during the Civil War. The Vicar of Acton, an adjoining parish, wrote in his diary: "On Saturday, they (the Royalists) came to Barthomley. As they marched they set upon the church, which had in it about twenty neighbours, that had gone in for safety; but the Lord Byron's troop, and Connaught, a major to Col. Sneyd, set upon them and won the church; the men fled into the steeple, but the enemy burning the forms, rushes, mats etc., made such smoke, that being almost stifled, they called for quarter, which was granted by Connaught; but when they had them in their power they stripped them them all naked, and most cruelly murdered twelve of them...Connaught cut the throat of Mr John Fowler, a hopeful young man, a minor, and only three of them escaped miraculously, the rest being cruelly wounded." But, as the church guide book points out: "In fairness, it must be said that the villagers were armed, and John Fowler, the rector's son, foolishy fired on the soldiers from the tower, killing one of their number and provoking revenge."

CLOGMAKER
*Joe Horrocks, a young
man following an old craft*
(24.3.92)

Kevin Barry O'Donnell

IRA sleeper in Shropshire
Secret arms dump not yet located

On Sunday, 16th February 1992, Barry O'Donnell led eight men in a one-minute machine gun attack against the RUC observation post and barracks at Coalisland, County Tyrone, Northern Ireland. There were no casualties on either side. The IRA group went to the nearby St. Patrick's Church car park at Clonnoe where they intended to dismantle the machine gun and make their escape in a get-away car. But the SAS knew their plan and had arranged an ambush. O'Donnell and three other terrorists were killed in a hail of bullets - 580 rounds were fired in the first 15 seconds. Two others were wounded and captured, and two escaped.

Somehow, Barry O'Donnell aroused a certain sympathy amongst the English public. Perhaps this is because he had never been connected to an incident involving civilian targets; perhaps because he was shot dead when he could have been captured alive. Certainly, his fellow students and his teachers at the Harper Adams College found this Gaelic-speaking young man likeable, quiet and charming and were deeply shocked to hear of his secret life and sudden death. In fact, he was a man born to die young. His parents are staunch Republicans and had named him Kevin Barry after their most famous martyr and hero of many Irish ballads.

The press cuttings overleaf outline his charmed but short life as an IRA terrorist (or freedom fighter, depending on your standpoint).

Bullets end 'charmed life'

By David Graves

KEVIN O'Donnell had lived a charmed life until he died in a hail of bullets after leading a machinegun attack on an Ulster police station. He had fooled an agricultural college, the police and an Old Bailey jury that he was not an IRA terrorist. But his luck ran out in a churchyard near his home town of Coalisland, Co Tyrone.

O'Donnell, who was 21 when he died, had been sent as a "sleeper" to Britain by the IRA in 1987 to study at Harper Adams agricultural college, near Newport, Shropshire.

While he cultivated a reputation as a quietly spoken, hard-working student his IRA masters used him as a "fetcher and carrier", taking arms and explosives to the organisation's so-called active service units around the country.

He was so successful in concealing his true identity that some of his fellow students even nicknamed him "The Bomber" as a joke. It was a cruel irony, but to many of them he was the last sort of person to be involved in terrorism.

O'Donnell's first stroke of luck came after the IRA bombing of the Clive Army barracks, Tern Hill, Shropshire, in February 1989. A getaway car used by the two terrorists who launched the bomb attack was abandoned 400 yards from the college.

Sixty of the college's 1,060

Continued on P2

Terrorists' student sleeper

Continued from P1

students came from Northern Ireland or the Irish Republic and all were closely interviewed by West Mercia detectives investigating the bombing. At the time of the attack O'Donnell was living in a hall of residence at the college. But he convinced the police he had nothing to do with the bombing.

Although police are now convinced there was a link between O'Donnell and the bombing they still do not know what it was — whether he was actually involved in the attack or had supplied the explosives to the bombers.

Soon afterwards Mrs Thatcher, then prime minister and one of the IRA's principal targets, visited the college. O'Donnell again evaded security checks on students.

Having escaped detection, O'Donnell, who was known as Barry by his fellow students, is thought to have played a key role in IRA attacks around the country.

He must have thought his luck had run out in May 1990, when he was arrested in north London after a high-speed car chase and two loaded Kalashnikov rifles were found in his Ford Cortina. Traces of explosives, including a Semtex component, were also found on his clothing and in the car. Detectives thought he had been caught red-handed before he could deliver the weapons.

The young terrorist refused to answer questions from anti-terrorist branch police and told the jury at his trial at the Old Bailey last March that he had been horrified to discover that the car, which he had left with a cousin in London, had been used by the IRA to store the rifles.

After an eight-day trial the jury believed him and his luck held. He was cleared.

Police on both sides of the Irish Sea were astonished by his acquittal.

The following month, back in Ulster, he was arrested in Coalisland after an RPG-7 rocket and a loaded rifle were found in a parked car. However, three weeks later he was freed after the prosecution withdrew charges.

"All the intelligence was that he went to town after his return and was very, very active," said an anti-terrorist police source.

Daily Telegraph
18.2.92

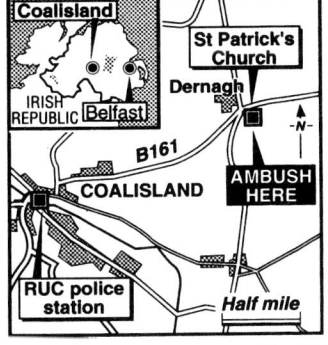

Lorry used in machine gun attack. O'Donnell died beside it

WILBROUGHTON HALL

Whilst studying agriculture at the Harper Adams College Barry O'Donnell lived with other students at Wilbroughton Hall. This is a neo-Jacobean mansion situated at the end of a long, straight lane that leads off the A518, Newport to Stafford road, at SJ.795.186. It stands on a bluff between a copse of pine trees and a yew-screened garden to the right, and its extensive farm buildings (dated 1831) to the left.

Wilbroughton Hall (21.2.92)

Just to the east is the route of the Roman road that connected Whitchurch to Stretton (near Penkridge), and just to the south is the disused track of the Newport to Stafford railway.

The house is not unhandsome, a red brick pile of three stories with stone dressings, gables, prominent chimneys and cast-iron latticed windows. The north gable is dated 1865 and from this side there are long views over the watery woods of the Aqualate estate. The south side of the house was probably the original front. It has less spectacular views but faces the sun.

ARMS CACHE

The countryside around is most attractive with many small woods and small marshes between the pastures and along the shores of the beautiful lake of Aqualate. The police anti-terrorist unit is convinced that there is at least one major arms and explosives cache hidden in the area. There have been intensive searches but, as yet, nothing has been found. The secret of its location lies buried with O'Donnell.

View NE from Wilbroughton Hall

Old Aqualate Hall designed by Nash, burned down in 1910

INDEX

Abbott's Castle 39
Acton 56
Afflow 38
Alsager 54
Altar, Elizabethan oak 54
Antoinette, Marie 48
Apwood Castle 39
Aqualate 61
Arms cache 61
Ashley 33
Astley 48-50
Astley's Ride, tune 48, 49
Aston Rogers 44
Bannock, Sergeant 51
Barry, Kevin 58
Barthomley 52-58
Benson, M P 45, 46
Bewdley 23
Black Heath 11
Boothen Road 24, 25
Boseley 10; Cloud 10;
  Reservoir 10, 11
Bovine walking frame 44
Bow Bells, carpenters 30
Bowerman, Tony 11
Bow-hauliers (men) 22, 23
Boyle, Kevin 41
Theatres of London 50
Bridestones 11
Bridgnorth 12
Brierley Hill 51
Bringewood Forge 29
Brindley, James 41
British Telecom 10
Bully Thrumble 10
Burman cat 7
Byron, Lord 56
CAMRA 53
Cartwright, Terry 53
Cats 6; Muffin 7; Gizmo 8
Cauldon Canal 14

Charlotte, Queen 50
Cheshire Plain 10
Chester, Earl of 11
Chief Constable of
  Staffordshire 46
Chosen Few 32
Circus 48, 50
Civil War 56
Clive Barracks 59
Clogmaker 57
Clonnoe 58
Cloudside 10
Coalisland 58, 59
Congleton 10
Connaught, Major 56
Continental Raiders 28
Coote, Mr 39
Cope, Audrey and Leslie 6, 7
Copeland, Richard Pirie,
  Ronald, and Emily 34
Crewe, family 53-55
Croker Hill 10
Culling foxhounds 26
Cuttlesdon 38
Daily Telegraph 59
Daisy Bank 55
Dana 14
Dane, River 10, 14
De Castro's Memoirs 50
Dernagh 59
Derrington 6, 31
Despencer, Hugh 14
Dial Lane 11
Dogs:
  Foxhounds 17, 26
  Staffordshire Bull-
  Terriers 16
  Ben 9
  Cindy 6
  Foxy 45
  Lady 9, In Memorium 9
  Mick the Black Country
  Gnasher 51
  Penny 6

Pirate 9, 36, 37
Queenie 45
Tess 36, 37
Twiggy 8
Dog and Lamp Post 51
Downton Castle 28
Doxey Brook 31
Drury Lane 50
Dublin 50
Duke of York 50
'Eagles', Stafford 32, 33
Earlsway, The 11
Elizabeth I 55
Elliott, General 50
Emsdorff 50
Endon 18
Evening Sentinel 24
Fir tree Cottage 53
Flash locks 22
Foster, family 39
Fowler, John 56
Foxhounds 26
Foxley 55
Franconi 50
Friedburg 50
Fulleshurst, Sir Robert 55
Gasholders 13
George III 48
Graves, David 59
Greek millionaire 28
Harper Adams College 58-60
Harroby, Earl 30
Haslington 54
Hatton, Sir Christopher 55
Hill Street, Brierley Hill 51
Hodson, Hilda 67
Horrocks, Joe 57
Hug Bridge 14
Hundreds 38
IRA 58, 59
Iron Age 11
John, King 16
Judicial gossipers 47
Judicial Review 46

Kalashnikov, rifle 59
Kibblestone 34
Lambeth 50
Leek 14
Leigh, John 45, 46
Llewellyn, Sam 22
London 59
Lonsdale Street 24
Lord Chancellor 46, 50, 55
Lud 14
Lyth Hill 42
Macclesfield 14; Canal 10
Magdalen 22
Mail Coach pub, Cliff Vale 32
Mainwearing, Master 20
Mareback 10
Mars 40
Martin, Ray and Reg 32
May Queen 18, 19
Merrymen 48
Middlewich 32
Moat Rough 39
Morris dancing 18
Nantwich 32
Nash, John 61
National Trust 10
Natural Sciences Centre 40
Newcastle-u-Lyme 48, 50
Newchapel 40, 41
New Inns, pub 51
Nicholls Street 24
Norman architecture 53, 55
North West Water 14
O'Donnell, Kevin
  Barry 58-60
Old Bailey 59
Olympic Pavilion theatre 50
Oulton 34
Pace, Michael and Tony
  40, 41
Paris 50
Pere-la-Chaise 50
Perjury 46
Pheasant and Partridge 20

Phillips, Fred 16
Pirehill 38
Praer, Family 54
Prima, Madam 29
Private station at Sandon 30
Pool Quay 23
Porthill 48
Potteries Link Road 52
Powell, Lord Baden 34
Punchbowl 53
Raven, Michael 33
Raven Rock 10
Real Ale 54
Rushton Spencer 14
Roberts, Barry 44
Royal Grove Theatre 50
RUC 58, 59
Rudyard, Lake 14
SADPALS 6, 36
Saint Bertoline 53, 55
Saint James, Newchapel 41
Saint Patrick 58, 59
Sand and gravel quarries 38
Sandon 30
Satellite weather pictures 40
SAS 58, 59
Saxons 38
Scouts 34
Seisdon 38
Semtex 59
Seven Stars, Seisdon 39
Severn, River 22, 23
Severn Trent Water 24
Sewers 24
Shaw, Dave 15
Shooting, game birds 20
Shropshire County Ranger 42
Smestow Brook 12, 38
Smirke, Sir Robert
Smithfield, London 50
Spode 34
Stafford 32, 33
Stoke on Trent 24, 32
Stourton Castle 16, 17

Stour, River 16
Stretton, Penkridge 61
Sugar Rock 10
Surrey Theatre 50
Swan Lane 13
Swans 27
Tarmac 38
Telford, Thomas 11
Tern Hill 59
Threat to Kill 45
Toad Hole 55
Tong 27
Totem-pole 35
Totmonslow 38
Trescott 12
Tressel, River 12
Trysull 38
Tyrone, County 58, 59
Ulster 59
Viking, space Ship 40
Walks in Mysterious Cheshire 11
Walnut Tree 55
Ward, Alf, of Whixall 43
War Stone 39
Water supply 14
Weirs 23
Well dressing 18
West Bromwich 13
Whiston Cross 17
Whitchurch 43, 61
White Lion, Barthomley 53, 54
Whitmore 20
Whixall Moss 43
Wilbroughton Hall 60
William I 14
Windsmoor Street 24, 25
Witness Summons 45
Wolverhampton 12
Wolves 153
Wooden theatres 50
The Worst Journey in the Midlands 22